OLD ABERBEEG & LLANHILLETH
IN PHOTOGRAPHS

by Bill Pritchard

OLD BAKEHOUSE PUBLICATIONS

ABERTILLERY

First published in January 1991

ISBN O 9512181 5 8

Published in the U.K. by
Old Bakehouse Publications
Church Street,
Abertillery, Gwent NP3 1EA
Telephone: 0495 212600 Fax: 0495 216222

Made and printed in the U.K.
by J.R. Davies (Printers) Ltd.

Foreword
by Mrs. Mary Edwards, B.Sc., J.P.

I feel sure that the production of this book by Bill Pritchard will bring back many happy memories to the people of Aberbeeg and Llanhilleth.

It is an enormous task to assemble the collection of photographs, many of them of buildings or views that no longer exist. Memories of the old Playhouse cinema and the problems of the traffic in the snow on the hills through the villages.

I feel that the book will provide a reminder of our heritage and will be sought after by the present residents and by the many people that now live in parts of the world, where their work has taken them.

My personal aquaintance of the author goes back many years, both as a resident and businessman. I wish him success in this and any future publication.

Acknowledgements

Acknowledgements are due to the undermentioned who kindly loaned their original material. Also, many thanks to those who helped identify faces, dates and details. I sincerely apologise for any names which have been inadvertently omitted.

Mrs. M. Preston, Mrs. Baber, Mrs. Trimm, Mrs. Lewis, Mrs. Gough, Mrs. Wall, Mrs. Stan Lewis, Mrs. Beames, Mrs. Brimble (nee Evans), Mrs. Day (Aberbeeg), Mrs. Peggy Giles, Mrs. McCarthey (nee Norris), Mrs B. Morris (nee Webber), Mrs. Violet Overfield, Mr. Jimmy Burton, Mr. Roy Johnson, Mr. Cyril Morgan, Mr. Harry Cotterill, Mr. Les Chivers, Mr. Arthur Prothero, Mr. Colin Weaver, Mr. Fred Parker, Mr. Lawrence Christie, Mr. Glyn Challenger, Mr. Ron Dykes, Mr. Ken Knowles, Mr. Arthur Kimber, Mr. Selway, Mr. Jack Bancroft, Committee Llanhilleth Institute, Mr. Wilf Forsey, Committee of Llanhilleth R.F.C., Mr. M. Neads, my brother Reg, Mr. M. Day (Canada), Mr. P. Dando, Mr. Selwyn Hancock, Mr. Howard Williams, Mr. D. Broome & Mr. Hurl.

Dedicated to Mam and Dad,
Jes and George
and
Nana Lacey

Introduction

My thanks to Mrs. M. Lloyd for these notes, the work of her husband Mr. Ken Lloyd Senior, Headmaster of Cwmtillery School, Abertillery (formerly a teacher at Aberbeeg School).

Llanhilleth, on old ordnance maps, is listed as Llanhiddel. St. Illtyd (Old Church) Gothic Church is without a tower or belfry, the bell is situated under the roof. In 1904 the church was surrounded by twelve yew trees and dedicated to St. Ithel.

In the early days of funerals at the church, it was expected that every man 'turn out' in order to carry the coffin, on a bier, up the steep lanes from the surrounding villages (Llanhilleth, Aberbeeg and Abertillery). The leading six bearers would travel twenty or thirty paces, rest, return to the end of the cortège and another six would take over, and this would be repeated every twenty or thirty paces. On arrival at the church gates, the leading six bearers, if not already in front, would take over. In later years Ralphs undertakers with their hearse and two black horses were used (Ralph later started a bus service) and for those who could afford a luxury in those days, a cab for the mourners. The rector of the church lived in Hafodyrynys, travelling on horseback to the church.

The Carpenters Arms, with its good stabling and accommodation was obviously a rest house for travellers. It is easy to assume that a public house in this location, was very handy. The proprietor in the early 1900s was Mrs. Taylor and from 1914-1947, Mrs. M. Hunt. Fifty yards up the road was another public house, The Castle Inn, which was only allowed to sell beer and not spirits. The proprietors were Mr. John and Jim Parfitt. It is now a private house.

As schoolboys we were able to point out what was supposed to be a part of the old Roman Road. We believed that the fortress at the rear of the Carpenters Arms was a Roman Outpost linked by a road to Caerleon and that the tumulus was a sentry post.

Since those days, however, my views have changed. Two friends of mine, Mr. Percy Jones and Mr. Trevor Lewis, as part of their research work while at Aberystwyth University, excavated this site and are of the opinion that it was a fortified house.

I believe that the tumulus was a beacon mound and this might bear investigation as from the summit, with the use of field glasses, can be seen another mound far away to the south west.

A few years ago a pupil at Aberbeeg school told me that when his father (Mr. Parfitt) was going to feed the chickens, the pathway collapsed and revealed a tunnel. This appeared to be travelling towards either the church or the fortified house.

On another occasion, a boy named Overfield brought a rusted sword to school, which he said had been recovered from a tunnel in one of the barns belonging to Argoed Farm.

These tunnels have caused a great deal of speculation as they seem to indicate passages towards St. Illtyd's.

Among the older inhabitants I have often heard it said that certain barns were used for services during the times of religious persecutions, and it needs little imagination to realise that these tunnels were escape routes.

St. Illtyd's Church was the original Parish Church of Llanhilleth, and the living was the preferment of the Marquis of Abergavenny. The late Rev. Daniel Felix was the last of this line and he told me that a knowledge of Welsh was essential before appointment to the living. It was then worth approximately £875, part of this being obtained in tithes. He lived at first in Hafodyrynys and later had the Church of St. Mark's built at Llanhilleth.

As the school at Aberbeeg was originally a church school, church services and sunday school were held there. Later a church was built on the left hand side of the hill as you travel towards Pentwyn. The flat (excavated) ground above the football field was the site. When Christchurch was built, this structure of corrugated zinc on the outside, was removed and taken to Crown Street, Crumlin.

As Christchurch and the rectory were erected in the Parish of Mynyddislwyn it needed a special dispensation to have them included in the Parish of Llanhilleth.

The bridge leading from Aberbeeg to Christchurch was always known as Mynyddislwyn Bridge.

Glandwr offers an interesting history. Baptisms were held in the river where the stream from Cwmnantygwynt joins the Ebbw. Looking up towards Cwmnant from the bridge, all that is left of a tram-road will be observed. From levels above this and along the mountain side towards Llanhilleth, a tram road brought coal which was sent down this incline and thereon to Crumlin where it was loaded onto barges.

Several places boast the name of 'The Jinney'. This is probably a corruption of jwrnai or journey as a tram road was called.

Perusal of the old log book at Aberbeeg school reveals a wealth of interesting history since 1873.

The school was leased to the Abertillery Education Committee at a nominal rent of £1 per annum conditional of certain rights to the Church. One meeting per week could be held without charge (the cleaner received 2/6 weekly from the Authority for cleaning afterwards) and the school could be used for parties at Whitsun and Christmas etc., with light and coal provided. The privilege is rarely used nowadays.

The pathway from Central Road, Llanhilleth was at one time known as Lovers Walk. Then the river was lined with trees and the mountainside abundantly covered with plantations etc.

Nowadays the pathway is lined with pigs' cots, the smells emanating from them hardly conducive to romance, except to the pigs.

The road from Aberbeeg to Abertillery originally went via 'Warm Turn'. Seventy years ago only a pathway led from 'Thomas' shop', through the woods, to Six Bells.

Prior to the erection of the new bridge the road led steeply down from the point where the Rhiw (Church Road) now joins the main Abertillery Road.

Aberbeeg Hospital was opened in 1923 with 40 beds. It was built at a cost of nearly £76,000. The Consulting Surgeon in charge was John Dunlop M.B., B.Ch., F.R.C.S. and Miss M. Downing was the Matron.

St. Mark's Church, Llanhilleth was erected in 1898 in stone in the Gothic style. It consisted of a chancel, nave, and a bell cote containing 2 bells with 350 sittings.

Christchurch, Aberbeeg was erected in 1910, in stone in the late 14th century style. It consisted of a chancel, nave, north and south transepts, aisles, organ chamber, vestry and tower at a cost of £6,000.

The rectory with a nett yearly income of £360, with residence is the gift of the Bishop of Monmouth, the Board of Patronage and the Provincial Board and has been held since 1930 by the Reverend Thomas Madog Williams B.A., of St. Davids College, Lampeter. By an order in council dated the 15th of December, 1911, Christchurch was substituted for that of St. Illtyd as a Parish Church.

Contents

FOREWORD

INTRODUCTION

ACKNOWLEDGEMENTS

CHAPTER 1   THE TWO VILLAGES AND THE
SURROUNDING SCENERY

CHAPTER 2   TRADE AND INDUSTRY

CHAPTER 3   MEMORABLE OCCASIONS AND GROUPS

CHAPTER 4   ENTERTAINMENT

CHAPTER 5   CARNIVAL TIME

CHAPTER 6   RELIGION

CHAPTER 7   EDUCATION

CHAPTER 8   TRANSPORT

CHAPTER 9   INDIVIDUAL CHARACTERS OF THE AREA

CHAPTER 10   SPORT AND LEISURE

CHAPTER 11   AND FINALLY...

CHAPTER 12   TRADESPEOPLE IN ABERBEEG AND
LLANHILLETH. CIRCA. 1934

CHAPTER 13   THE ABERBEEG TRAGEDY

CHAPTER 1

Llanhilleth, Aberbeeg and surrounding scenery

1. A picture of Llanhilleth Old School, taken from the horse shoe bend, circa 1905.

2. A photograph taken from Woodside Terrace at the rear of the Wesleyan Chapel. Bowens sweet shop and Flook the cobblers are at the centre of the picture, circa 1905.

3. Llanhilleth Colliery in the centre, Hafodycoed on the top left; both no longer exist. The River Ebbw is on the bottom left.

4. Commercial Road, the Conservative Club is now on the site of the first two houses on the left Circa 1905.

8

5. A general view of Llanhilleth. In the bottom left of the picture is Bowens sweet shop and Jack Flook the cobblers.

6. Llanhilleth. River Ebbw and Lovers Walk.

7. High Street and Maesycnew Terrace, Llanhilleth, with the railway stock for the colliery in the foreground.

8. Llanhilleth hill and on the right the turning into Brooklyn Terrace.

9. St. Marks Church, circa 1930.

10. Notorious Llanhilleth hill in the winter snow, with the Wesleyan Chapel in
the foreground.

11

View up Valley, Llanhilleth

11. A view of the valley of Llanhilleth. Note there is no Cae-felin Street or Partridge Road. Brynhyfryd School was just being built.

12. Commercial Street, with the Central Hotel the first building on the left.

13. Christchurch, Aberbeeg with Glandwr Street in the foreground.

14. Llanhilleth Rectory, Aberbeeg.

15. Another view up the valley of Llanhilleth with allotments on the left and Glandwr Chapel in the centre. Also in the picture is the marshalling yard used for the goods trucks in Tudors Field. This is now the industrial estate.

16. General view of Aberbeeg circa 1930. In the centre of the picture is the old tin chapel. The author erected the petrol filling station in 1952 on this site followed by the complete garage. Also in the picture are Rhiw Cottages and the marshalling yard. The old River Ebbw run was changed to prevent flooding at Glandwr, Aberbeeg.

17. New Parish Church, Aberbeeg. Note no grave stones.

18. River Ebbw and pathway, Llanhilleth.

19.   The Ivorites, Aberbeeg.

20.   High Street, Llanhilleth circa 1939. Note the unusual lamp posts -
telegraphic or electric?

21. Aberbeeg Pit.

22. The rolling stock at Llanhilleth Colliery.

23. Old Woodland Terrace, Aberbeeg. In the picture is a horse and cart which belonged to 'Days the Baker', the makers of Carr's Malt Bread, which is advertised on the rear.

24. High Street, Llanhilleth, with Ware's shop in the foreground.

25. A general view of Llanhilleth. In the foreground is the site on which the new by-pass road has been built. Also in the picture is the Playhouse Cinema and the station platform.

26. Aberbeeg Square.

CHAPTER 2

Trade and Industry

27. W.J. Herbert, Grocer,
High Street, Llanhilleth.

28. A. Hunt, Saddler, Commercial Road, Llanhilleth.

29. Thos. Day, Baker and Confectioner (father of Joe Day), Aberbeeg, 1918, High Street, Llanhilleth (next to the police station).

30. Joe Day in 1912 when he was 8 years old. This business finally became James and Day, Baker and Confectioners, Aberbeeg.

31. An India and China Tea Shop, Commercial Road, Llanhilleth in 1920. One of the ladies outside the shop was named Helen.

32. The Walpole Hotel, Llanhilleth. Bill Phillips was the landlord, circa 1930. A man named 'one arm Jes' also used to work there, with whom the author used to go on a horse and cart, delivering bottles of beer etc. around the houses. It is now the home of Llanhilleth R.F.C.

33. The Hanbury Hotel, Aberbeeg. Sadly, demolished in 1990.

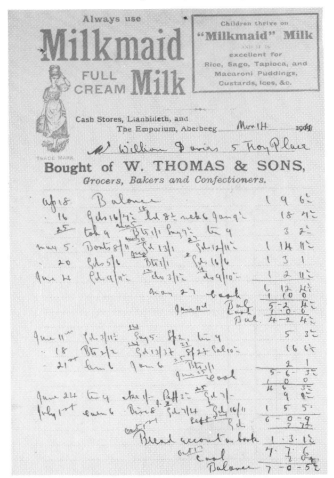

34. An invoice used by The Cash Stores, Llanhilleth and The Emporium, Aberbeeg dated March 14th, 1910.

35. A 1949 outing of the Grocers Association to Cadbury Bros. Ltd., Bournville.

CHAPTER 3

Memorable Occasions and Groups

36. An outing to Caswell Bay in July 1940.

37. Llanhilleth ladies outing in 1938.

38. Aberbeeg Club outing.

39. Jones Buses, Aberbeeg. Presentation of Long Service Awards to Archie Hinder, J. Dyke, O. Langley, S. Jones and D. Simmonds. In the front of the picture is Sarge Warren (Inspector).

ESTABLISHED 1838.

WEBB'S (ABERBEEG) LIMITED
BREWERS AND WINE AND SPIRIT MERCHANTS
ABERBEEG, MON.

Centenary Celebration 1938

The Directors of Webb's (Aberbeeg) Ltd., invite their Staff, Employees and their Wives to an Excursion to the Empire Exhibition, Scotland, 1938, at Glasgow, on Saturday, June 11th, 1938.

P. T. O.

40/41. An invitation from Webb's Brewery directors to their staff for a visit to the Empire Exhibition in Glasgow to celebrate the brewery's centenary in 1938.

Train leaves ABERBEEG on Friday, June 10th, 1938, at 9.30 p.m. and will leave Newport at 10.30 p·m.

Arriving at Glasgow (Buchanan Street) at 8.20 a.m. on Saturday, June 11th.

Breakfast will be provided free at the Ca'doro Restaurant, 122 Union Street, Glasgow, at 9 a.m.

The railway tickets cover the journey and admission to the Exhibition.

Frequent trains run from Glasgow to the Exhibition.

Train leaves GLASGOW (Buchanan Street) for Aberbeeg at 1.0 a.m. on Sunday, June 12th, 1938.

42. A line up of the brewery staff at the time of the centenary, 1938.

1838 WEBB'S (ABERBEEG) LTD CENTENARY CELEBRATION 1938

CHILDRENS' EXCURSION TO BARRY ISLAND AUGUST 9TH 1938

43. A group of employees' children about to embark on a trip to Barry Island on
9th August, 1938.

44.   A Jones staff party for the retirement of Sam James at the Ironside Club, Tredegar.

45. Llanhilleth men on a trip to Blackpool. Back row left to right: Jose Webber, Morgan, Unknown, Unknown, Woodland. Middle row left to right: J. Carter, Connolly, C. Hagland, T. Withers, T. Chivers, Unknown, Unknown. Front row left to right: A. Brown, Bill Parry, Shad Davies, Pound, Challenger, Whitlock.

Entertainment

46. 1947 Llanhilleth Excelsior Male Voice Choir. Left to right: I. Jones,
E. Dykes, J. Dykes, G. Halford, Unknown, A. Baber, C. Maxwell, P. Maggs,
E. Pratley, C. Morgan, E. Evans, J. Frost, T. Holbrook. J. Bryant is the pianist
and H. Crawford the conductor.

47. July 1953, Abertillery Carnival Queen was Margery Lewis of Llanhilleth.

48. Illtyd Operatic Society in 1958 with their version of Gypsy Baron. The principals are A. Carter Jnr., Mr. Carter Snr., E. Watts, P. Hurl and M. Simmonds.

49. Illtyd Operatic Society in 1928. In the picture are Tom Hurl, J. Lewis (Thatch), H. Crawford, J. Wilcox, R. Morgan, D. Lewis, T. Angel and Kate Thomas.

50. The Playhouse Cinema.

It was about the year 1910 that work began on preparing the site of the Playhouse or as it was originally intended to be named 'The Hippodrome'.

To prepare the site meant moving the solid rock which had to be blasted out with explosives and it was thought that this solid foundation would last forever. The blasting operation was a great attraction to the children.

At the time the Playhouse was built, lighting by electricity was in its early stages in this area.

To supply electric power to the Playhouse a generating set was housed in the basement of the building. Much of the work of installing wiring and switches was carried out by the late Mr. William John Harris who, at the time, lived in Hillside Terrace, Llanhilleth and earned his living as a shoe repairer in a small wooden building which was at the end of Hillside Terrace.

When the building was completed, the entertainment, which was provided by touring companies of actors and actresses, attracted many people from all parts of the valleys.

The school children also occasionally provided a week of concerts, as did the male voice choirs. The Illtyd Operatic Society also gave choral and operatic performances, each of which was performed for a week at a time to a packed audience.

In the early days, silent films were provided at the Workmen's Institute, but by the early 1930s talking films had become the thing of the day and the Playhouse went over to being a cinema.

This went on for about 20 years, then in the 1950s when television became popular the crowds began to decline and the usefulness of the cinema ceased.

The beginning of the bingo rage gave it a new lease of life, but this was only to be short lived.

The mining coal seams underneath the Playhouse weakened the whole ground including the solid rock on which the Playhouse had been built. Many efforts were made to save the building but they were of no use. The foundations had been weakened so much that the building became dangerous, and had to be pulled down to ground level.

51. The Llanhilleth Illtyd Operatic Society presenting Countess Maritza in 1956. Back row left to right: E. Saunders, M. Simmonds, A. Carter, G. Pope, H. Carter, P. Carter, J. Horseman and J. Carter. Front row left to right: M. Morgan and G. Morgan.

52. Excelsior Male Voice Choir, 1931.

53. Llanhilleth Jazz Band, 1949. Back row left to right: D. Reed, M. Bryant, Unknown, M. Connolly, J. Woodland, J. Matthews, M. Morgan, B. Webber. Front row: Bogsy Woodward, Lewis, N. Bray, E. Jones, J. Parker, P. Dennis, B. Bryant, H. Chivers, P. Watkins.

54. Llanhilleth Choir, 1930. Back row left to right: B. Sansom, A. Hurl, T. George, F. Jones, Joe William, Phil Bevan, Tom Hurl and Eddie Davies. Middle row left to right: Benham, J. Lewis, Joe Wilcox, Jack Dykes, W. Harwood, G. Watkins, W. Harris and C. Reed. Front row left to right: A. Norris, W. Forsey, T. Angel, H. Crawford (Conductor), V. Rideout, Jim Lewis, B. Smart and A. Barber.

CHAPTER 5

Carnival Time

55. Carnival time at Troy Road. In the picture are H. Ware, Jack Minchington, Snook, Bryn Davies, Chedsey, Dick Lewis, Sam Smithy and Tom Jones.

56. Carnival time.

57. Carnival time.

58. Llanhilleth Jazz Band in 1951 with Mr. Webber as their trainer.

59. Mrs. Norris of Brooklyn Terrace.

60. Carnival time.

61. Carnival float from Maesycnew Terrace in 1953. Left to right:
Sylvia Gough, Mrs. Wall, I. Chivers, K. Belcher, J. Jones, J. Wall, E. James and
Mrs. Keeling.

62. Carnival time.

63. Troy Road carnival entry, 1951. Mrs. Lewis, Mrs. Ashford, Mrs. Plaister and Co.

64. The placards say 'we did our bit to secure victory'. Commercial Road.

65. Elsie Jones, Joyce Parker and Co.

66. Carnival time.

67. Meadow Street's carnival entry.

68. Carnival time.

69. Meadow Street, Hula, Hula. With Nora Lane on the right, also in the picture are Jimmy Burton and Joan Peck.

70. Troy Road, Blaencuffin Road and Hafodarthen Road at carnival time. In the picture are A. Plaister, Bryn Davies, Mrs. Ware, Sam Smithy, V. Lewis, G. Probyn, Lucy Lucas, Snook, E. Butler, M. Plaister, Price, Mrs. Cannon, Mrs. Davies and Mrs. Ashford.

CHAPTER 6

Religion

71. Glandwr Chapel.

72. Glandwr Baptist Church, Llanhilleth. Centenary 1838/1938, pastor and deacons. Pastor Rev. C.O. Price. Deacons F.G. Phillimore, Gomer Jones, Thomas Phillips, W.M. Taylor, James Mead, S.T. Harris, A. Parry and George Jones.

73. Members of the Glandwr Baptist Church taken at the 21st anniversary celebrations of the new chapel in 1927.

74. The Zion Chapel Whitsun Walks at High Street, Llanhilleth with J. Aldred Evans (the vicar), and Mr. Buchan from Commercial Road in the foreground.

75. The Zion Chapel Bazaar.

76. Llanhilleth Baptist Church, Commercial Road on their Whitsun Walk with Mr. Jones the minister.

77.   The School Walks. In the picture are Jack Dykes, Don Norris, Jack Flook
and Mr. Carpenter.

78.   Baptist Church, Commercial Road on their Whitsun Walk in 1926.
Hunt Bros. saddlers shop is in the background on the left.

79.   1915 Commercial Road Baptist, Sunday School Walks.

80.   Sunday School outing from Commercial Road Baptist Church in 1927. In the picture Partridge Road is on the left.

81. Tabernacle Sunday School, Aberbeeg on their outing. Approx. 1914.

82. Taken in 1927 the Forward Movement on the bridge with Tudors Field on the right.

83. 1924 Zion Choir, Whitsun Walks.

84. 1924 Commercial Road Baptist Church Whitsun Walks. In the background you can see Holmes Cafe and the gents Tailors/Drapers. There was no post office at this date.

85. Whitsun Walks, Forward Movement approx. 1914/21.

86. Presbyterian Sunday School at High Street, Llanhilleth with Jack Dykes second from the left and Mr. Benham third from the left.

87. Llanhilleth Zion Chapel. Back row left to right: T. Hewitt, F. Hewitt and Tom Belcher. Front row left to right: T. Crockett, C. Owen and J. Pearce.

88. Glandwr Sunday School, 1938. Pastor, Officers and Teachers. Insets left to right: H.Crawford, A. Mead, E. Harris, A. Snook and Mr. E. Phillimore. Standing left to right: A. Parry, G. Crawford, B. Giles, B. Challenger, T. Tanner, C. Chedsey and W. Wilhelm. Seated left to right: Mr. and Mrs. Taylor, Mrs. Price, Rev. P.O. Price, G. Jones, P. Giles, Mrs. Chedzey and A. Parry.

89. The old Glandwr Chapel which was built in 1838.

90. St. Illtyd Church, an excellent reproduction by local artist G.G. Gullick of Six Bells.

CHAPTER 7

Education

91. The first Baptist Church School in 1880. On the extreme right in the back row is William Wheeler, then the foreman of Abertillery Council. The school headmaster in the centre was J. Rowlands. The photograph was taken in Llanhilleth Park when it was surrounded by trees.

92. Llanhilleth Old School Infants in 1963.

93. Llanhilleth Mixed School, Standard 6.

94. Brynhyfryd Infants School around 1931.

55

95. Brynhyfryd School, 1919. The teachers are Miss Thomson and Miss Watson.

96. Aberbeeg Junior School, 1927.

97. Ty-Graig School, 1959.

98. Llanhilleth Old School, Standard 1.

99. Llanhilleth Old School, 1959. The teacher is Miss Roberts.

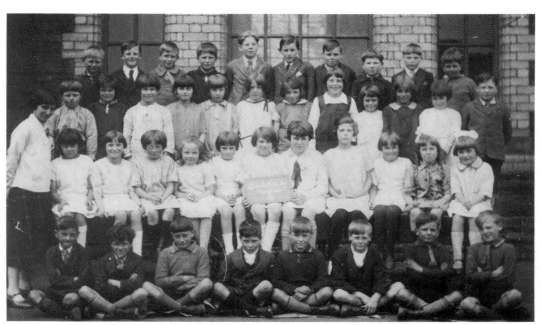

100. Llanhilleth Old School, Standard 4.

101. Llanhilleth Old School.

102. Brynhyfryd School in 1937. Back row left to right: Thoral Forward,
Arthur Martin, George Angel, Glyn Cornet and Bill Pritchard (the author).
Front row left to right: Glyn Morgan, Roy Mapp, Idris Davies, Jack Bancroft
and Trevor Jones.

103. Ty-Graig School 1927, Standard 3A. Some of the faces in the picture are Woodward, Rogers, V. Williams, Jones, B. Nichols, Mayo, S. Weaver, W. Head, Howells, E. James, V. Edwards, D. Morgan, R. Moore, Challenger, Rowles.

104. Ty-Graig School year 1958/59. The teachers are Miss Stone and Miss Burge.

105. Brynhyfryd School, 1927. Faces include E. Jackson, C. Sanson, E. Thomas, R. Evans, Goode, M. Carter, Clark, Mildred Barry, M. Williams, E. Barrett, M. Paget, L. Salter, K. Davies, H. Hurl, Webster, D. Lane, Kempthorne.

106. Llanhilleth Old School, 1928-29. Harold Jones was the teacher. Back row left to right: Unknown, Jayne, Unknown, Unknown, Olga Belcher, Unknown, Tom Johnson, Doug Jones, Cyril Morgan and Evans. Third row left to right: Morris, Glyn Hawkins, Harry Owen, Hynam, Selina Morgan, W. Gale, J. Williams, J. Exton, J. Bowen, M. Neads and L. Burchell. Second row left to right: Johnson, B. Walker, Unknown, Ruby Edmunds, Unknown, Unknown, B. Bevan, Unknown, L. Carey, Unknown, and Grosvenor. Front row left to right: Andrews, H. Hewings, David Lewis, Unknown, Bernard Goddin, Archie Bailey, Haydon Duffield, Cyril Davies and Needham Taylor.

107. Back row left to right: V. Brunt, teacher Ty-Graig School, L. Brunt, clerk on GWR and B. Brunt a teacher at Brynhyfryd School. Front row left to right: M. Brunt, C. Brunt and T. Brunt.

108. Ty-Graig School, 1922.

109. Llanhilleth Old School, Class 5.

110. Llanhilleth Old School, Standard 3 in 1939 with Mr. Bowen, the teacher.

CHAPTER 8

Transport

111. This picture was taken in 1927 on the Cwm to Hafodyrynys bus route. The owner of the Green Bus Service was Anthony Overfield, who sold it to the Valley Bus Service. In the picture is Kenneth Overfield.

112. A trip to Porthcawl on 19th August, 1934 with Mr. G.Jones, the driver.

113. This picture of Albert Prior, Traffic Manager of Jones Buses, was taken in 1938.

114. Mr. Dark, General Manager of National Buses, presents a coach to Jones Preservation Staff in 1976. In the picture is J. Badcott, M. Williams, S. Hancock and Tom Cornick (Inspector).

115. The last train from Aberbeeg Station in 1962. Left to right: H. Moore, Mrs. James, B. Godwin and J. Northey.

116. Aberbeeg Station, left to right B. Hill, P. Giles, P. Tong and Mrs. James.

117/118. Two photographs of the New Filling Station, Aberbeeg.

119. An insert from Goodyear Tyre Company magazine in 1956.

This garage, the New Filling Station, is located in the Abertillery valley, on a site at present being developed by carving the required space out of the rock face. Not by the modern means of rock drilling equipment and blasting; this was considered to be too hazardous in view of the proximity of petrol tanks. Instead, a determined and experienced man has removed hundreds of tons of solid rock - by hammer and chisel alone.

His first job was to produce a crater 13 ft x 9 ft x 12 ft deep to house two tanks for the electric pumps installed - and, when weather permitted, he continued the job of site clearance with the result that he has cut over 1,000 tons of solid rock - all of which, incidentally, has been sold to a local quarry for crushing.

The man who quietly and effectively undertook this mammoth task is Mr. Charlie Easton, who spent many years of his life in coal mining, as a borer.

Mr. Bill Pritchard, proprietor of the New Filling Station, is very proud of him and the job he has done.

With good reason! For Charlie Easton is 81 years old.

120. Jones Bus on the Crumlin via Trinant route. In the background is Aberbeeg showing the old goods yard, Methodist Chapel and Warm Turn.

121.   A Jones Bus at Aberbeeg Social Club. The old buildings on the left at the rear were the stables and the surgery of Dr. Scanlon.

122.   A proficiency drivers presentation to Ron George. Left to right: Postmaster Unknown, T. Blake, Ron George and Supt. Baker.

CHAPTER 9

Individual characters of the area

123. Origin of picture unknown. It is said to have been taken during the miners strike, 1925.

124. Albert Baber and Bess Blackmoor as they appeared in Iolanthe by Gilbert and Sullivan.

125. Albert Baber Junior as we all knew him.

126. A picture of the 2nd Monmouthshire T.A.s 1939/45. In the picture are Captain Ken Treasure, S. Crease, Bill Preston, Bill Neale and Wilf Williams.

127. Harry & Olwen Holmes.

128. Aberbeeg Hospital, 1958 or 1959. Standing left to right: Dr. Scanlon and Mr. Aubrey (Charge Nurse). Seated left to right: Sisters Stevens, Prosser, Matron Body, Sisters Lewis and Poultney.

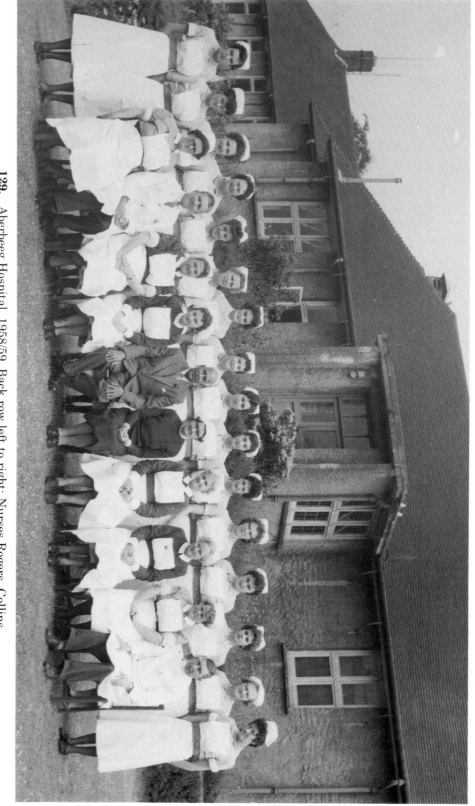

129. Aberbeeg Hospital, 1958/59. Back row left to right: Nurses Rogers, Collins, Purnell, Unknown, Nash, Jenkins, R. Jones, S.E.N. Janes, Nurses Haycock, H. Jones, S. Bowditch, S.E.N. Judge, Nurses Price, M. Morgan, Priddy and Perry. Front row left to right: Staff Nurse Meredith, Mr. Aubrey, Sisters Stevens, Prosser, Dr. Scanlon, Matron Body, Sisters Lewis, Poultney, Staff Nurse Hopkins and Mr. Cleaton.

130. Albert Baber Senior who was the cobbler at the rear of Caefelin Street. He died in 1944 aged 68 years.

131. 1961 Civil Defence Welfare Competition Winners, Aberbeeg Division. Standing left to right: Mrs. Harris and Mrs. Day. Seated left to right: Unknown, Mrs. Newman, Mrs. Meyrick and Mrs. Burnet.

133. Aberbeeg Hospital Staff. Back row left to right: Mr. Temple (Physio), Mr. Martindale (Boilerman and Sterilising Attendant), Mr. Atkins (Gardener) and Mr. G. Pyle (X ray). Middle row left to right: Miss D. Webley (Domestic), Nurses Hookings, Greenhouse, Plummer, Miss H. Watkins, P. Thomas (Domestic), Mr. Heighway (Electrical & Maintenance Engineer), Miss Purnell (Secretary), Nurses Long, Bayliss, R. Jones, M. Palmer, Morgan, Mrs. Lewis (Seamstress), Mr. Pritchard (Charge Nurse) and Miss J. Florence (Domestic). Front row left to right: Sisters Lewis, Adams, lady friend of Matron Body, Matron Body, Canon Madog Williams, Sisters Harris and Longhurst.

134.　The 2nd Monmouthshire T.A.s. Included in this picture are
Shoc. Edwards, Prosser, Cuckoo Young, Erin Carter, Ivor Trim, E. Snook,
E. Mann, T. Bray and E. Rogers.

135.　Mr. Rees of Hyde Place, the official council 'ratcatcher', seen here with his
dog, ferret and a rat.

136. Abertillery District Cub Camp 1952. Scout Master T. Lewis.

137. Mr. & Mrs. Edmund Jones and family in 1952.

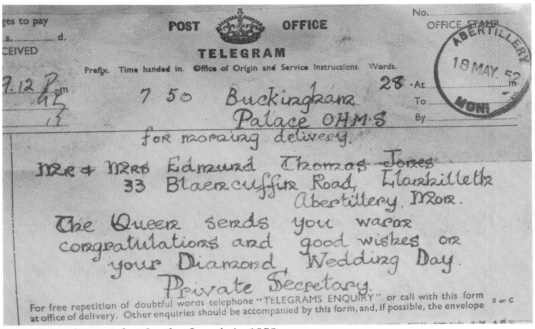

POST · OFFICE

TELEGRAM

Prefix. Time handed in. Office of Origin and Service Instructions. Words.

7 50 Buckingham
Palace OHMS
for morning delivery.

Mr & Mrs Edmund Thomas Jones
33 Blaencuffin Road, Llanhilleth
Abertillery. Mon.

The Queen sends you warm
congratulations and good wishes on
your Diamond Wedding Day.
Private Secretary.

For free repetition of doubtful words telephone "TELEGRAMS ENQUIRY" or call with this form
at office of delivery. Other enquiries should be accompanied by this form, and, if possible, the envelope

138. A great day for the Jones's in 1952.

139. Mr. & Mrs. Edmund Jones celebrating their Diamond Wedding in 1952.

140. Stormy weather - 1931 style. Four Llanhilleth families lost their homes in a freak storm sixty years ago. One of the women, Mrs May Watkins (then Mrs Smith) was expecting her first child and had to be rescued from her waterlogged home by the local police sergeant. The flooded houses were all at High Street, near the old pithead baths. The Caullander, Challenger and Foxwell families also lost their homes.

CHAPTER 10

Sport and Leisure

141. Llanhilleth R.F.C., Cyrus Davies Cup Winners around 1943. Back row left to right: Morgan, Arthur Gwillyn, Padmore, M. Jayne, A. Prothero, G. Angel, Unknown, L. Carey, Unknown, J. Coleman, Alf Hayer, Unknown. Middle row left to right: J. Davies, S. Smithy, Hopkins, J. Phelps, Unknown, K. Connolly, J. Evans, Eatwell, Bill Preston. Front row left to right: Unknown, I. Mounter and Ray Hardacre.

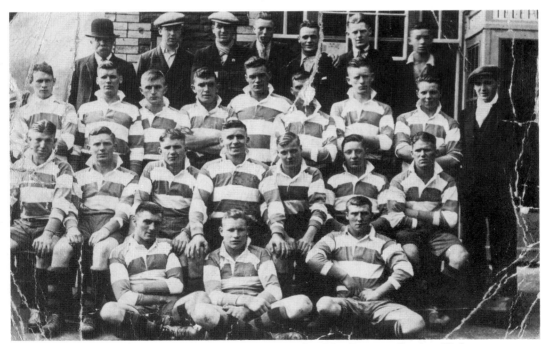

142. Llanhilleth R.F.C. Back row left to right: Mr. Preston Senior, Unknown, B. Jayne, M. Evans, Mr. Preston Junior, C. Lewis, J. Lewis. Third row left to right: G. Williams, I. Thomas, H. Jayne, Challenger, A. Prothero, Snooks, O. Lewis, D. Butcher, Jayne. Second row left to right: Unknown, S. Lewis, G. Eatwell, G. Smithy, Unknown, D. Lewis, T. Thomas. Front row left to right: C. Pritchard, D. Jones and Benson.

143.   Llanhilleth Albion A.F.C.

144.   Llanhilleth R.F.C. 1955. In the picture are M. Neads, C. Samson,
B. Samson, E. Pople, W. Jones, J. Watkins, M. Whitlock, B. Coleman, W. Hodges,
V. Davies, L. Hagland and D. Watts.

145. Llanhilleth Junior Rugby 1952/53. Back row left to right: S. Jones, Francombe, Compton, Unknown, D. Blanche, D. Blackpool, G. Mann, T. Minchin. Middle row left to right: B. Challenger, Unknown, T. Wilkins, Tovey, G. Garlini. Front row left to right: Mocker Attwell, G. Carter, Unknown, T. Barry and M. Gresham.

146. Jones F.C., Aberbeeg. Standing left to right: K. Overfield, A. Jones, T. Thomas, R. Barton, M. Sweet, D. Jayne, C. Jones and A. Hockey. Front row left to right: M. Owen, A. Carter, S. Smith, T. Saunders and P. Harvey.

147. Quoits match at Waunlwyd, Ebbw Vale. In the picture are Alf Donald Senior, I. Carter, W. Parry, L. Dennis, W. Vaughan, M. Watkins, F. Brown, B. Jenkins, E. Stock, Mr. Connelly and A. Parker.

148. Llanhilleth Bowlers. Back row fourth from left: Mrs. Nathan Lewis. Middle row: first left Mr. Arthur Morgan, fifth from left Mr. Alf Thayer. Front row: second from left Mr. Nathan Lewis (Curly), third from left Mr. Tom Ansel.

149. Colin Weaver, the Welsh professional sprinter. Colin started his professional training at the age of 9. In the days leading up to a big race (Powderhall) his morning diet was to drink raw eggs and sherry. He then went onto a private track to perfect his sprinting technique, after that he had a massage followed by a game of cards and then his nightcap was another dose of raw eggs mixed with port, before he went to bed at 9 pm.

He competed in 8 Powderhall finals including 4 Scottish finals at which his results were 2nd in 1935, 5th in 1937, 2nd in 1943 and 2nd in 1946.
He competed in the Welsh final in 1931.

In later years, Colin became trainer to many running and rugby stars.

150. Reg Weaver, the winner of the English Powderhall 1943 at Cooraidge Stadium, Stoke on Trent. Also in the picture were the Lord Mayor, his wife and the event promoter.

151. E. Morgan, the 1925 winner of the Welsh 130 yards Powderhall. He won £100 and a gold medal.

152. Reg Weaver, the 1943 winner of the English Powderhall Championship.

153. Back row left to right: L. Carpenter, J. Lewis, J. Hodder, Rees, Boiler Evans, V. Davies, Nicky Jones, D. Watts, Blanche, Broome and S. Butler. Front row left to right: J. (Patch) Lewis, Dinky Davies, Lane, B. Sainsbury, B. Hill, J. Summers and R. Tarlin.

154. Llanhilleth Institute Team. Back row left to right: Len Carpenter, Jim Lewis, Jimmy Hodder, Broome and Stan Butler. Seated left to right: J. (Patch) Lewis, R. Tarlin, B. Sainsbury, Bert Hill and Johnny Summers.

155. Brynhyfryd Netball Team 1952/53. Standing left to right: D. Watts, J. Davies, A. Newcombe and S. Butler. Seated left to right: Unknown, I. Beddis and P. Hale.

156. Parry Dando, the 1952 Light Welter Weight Welsh Champion, British Coal Board Champion and British and Welsh International.

157. 1944/45 Aberbeeg Junior School Relay Team. Standing left to right: Unknown and S. Denning. Seated left to right: M. Jukes and Bees.

158. Llanhilleth Bowling Club, included in the picture are Ted Evans, Alf Mapp, Nathan Lewis, Phil Harris, Rowlands, Jos Chivers, Bob Angel and Mr. Wall.

159. Aberbeeg Darts 4-a-side 1963/64 Hospital Cup Winners. Standing left to right: J. Worthey, C. Maggs and F. Hinton. Seated left to right: N. Strickland, A. Strong, C. Chivers and E. Howells.

160. The British Boxing Team at the 1952 Olympic Games. Parry Dando in the company of Dai Dower (Cardiff), Flyweight and Henry Cooper (London), Light Heavy Weight.

BRITAIN'S BOXING TEAM FOR THE OLYMPIC GAMES 1952

WEIGHT	TEAM	RESERVES
Fly	D. Dower (Roath Youth, Cardiff)	J. Smillie (Scotland)
Bantam	T. G. Nicholls (Sankey's Wellington)	R. Jenkins (Wales)
Feather	P. J. Lewis (Royal Air Force)	P. Brander (Slough)
Light	F. Reardon (Downham, London)	R. Hinson (Army)
Light–Welter	P. Waterman (Caius, London)	P. Dando (Wales)
Welter	J. P. Maloney (R.A.F. and Dagenham)	T. C. Budge (Wales)
Light–Middle	B. Foster (Mitchells & Butlers, B'ham.)	B. Wells (Royal Air Force)
Middle	T. Gooding (Army & G.B.K.N., Cardiff)	K. Phillips (Worley)
Light–Heavy	H. Cooper (Eltham, London)	D. Rowe (Royal Air Force)
Heavy	E. Hearn (Battersea, London)	M. B. Cowen (Battersea)

President of the Amateur Boxing Association :
H. G. H. CHANDLEY ESQ.

Hon. Secretary of the A.B.A. :
JAS. O. MCINTOSH ESQ.

Team Manager : H. W. MALLIN

Assistant Team Manager : T. PARKINSON

Trainer : A. GALLIE

Assistant Trainer : Sergt. Major Inst. F. VERLANDER (A.P.T.C.)

Referees : S. ROYLE, C. THOMPSON

BRITISH OLYMPIC GAMES CHAMPIONS

1908—London	1920—Antwerp
Bantam—H. Thomas	*Middle*—H. W. Mallin
Feather—R. K. Gunn	*Heavy*—R. R. Rawson
Light—F. Grace	
Middle—J. W. H. T. Douglas	
Heavy—A. L. Oldham	

1924—Paris
Middle—H. W. Mallin
Light-heavy—H. J. Mitchell

161. Llanhilleth Cricket Club 1958/59. Back row left to right: Mr. Thayer,
D. Cunvin, R. Cross, C. Dyke, A. Sargeant, K. Hall, J. Cunvin, J. Newberry,
Mr. Carter. Middle row left to right: R. Rogers, R. Ashmead, P. Maggs (Capt.),
K. Musto and J. Morgan. Front row left to right: J. Butcher and P. Bryant.

162. Llanhilleth Cricket Club 1967/68. Back row left to right: E. Dyke,
T. Hayward, G. Challent, K. Hall, C. Belcher, P. Maggs, O. Rogers. Middle row
left to right: R. Ashmead, R. Royger, D. Butcher (Capt.), B. Lewis, G. Ashmead.
Front row left to right: G. Dyke, R. Lewis and J. Haywood.

163. Aberbeeg Cricket Committee and some of the team pictured in the late 1920s. In the back row third from the left is Lionel Thomas and, seated second on the right John Dixon, Chairman of Webbs Brewery.

164. Llanhilleth Cricket Team, 1898. On the top left of the picture is Harry Creed. Geo Rogers is third from the right in the back row and Reg Williams is the second on the left in the centre row.

165. Llanhilleth Town Cricket Club. Monmouthshire Cricket Association League Cup joint winners 1967. Back row left to right: R. Ashmead, D. Davies, K. Musto, C. Belcher, R. Lewis, S. Lewis and B. Lewis. Front row left to right: A. Sargeant, W. Butler, E. Matthews (Capt.), P. Maggs, M. Sweet.

166. 1920 Quoits. In the picture are Lane, Penn, Jos Chivers, William Morgan, Jack Rogers, Speedy Thayer, Joseph Burton, Robert Christian and Bill Chivers.

167. The Welsh Quoits team at Llanhilleth. In the picture are Ron Evans, Alf Nash, Jack Price, Bill Bray, W. Price, F. Parker, C. Winstone, P. Lloyd, J. James, O. Stephens, R. Palmer, B. Hayes, A. Baker (Sec.) and D.R. Williams.

Fred Parker is Welsh champion

FRED PARKER, of Llanhilleth, is again the Welsh quoiting champion. In the semi-finals, played at Llanhilleth, he beat his brother, Alfred, by 51 points to 13, and in the final, at Waunlwyd, which was marred by rain and gale-force wind, he accounted for E. Stocks, 61-42.

Stocks had surprisingly beaten E. Robinson in the semi-final.

Fred Parker maintained his excellent form by defeating C. Jenkins 31-15 in the second round of the Mills cup at Llanhilleth. He will meet W. Warren in the semi-finals at Oakdale next Saturday. Ron Palmer has been drawn against W. Hughes. The final will also be played on Saturday.

Play starts at four o'clock, and the referee is Mr. E. Robinson.

In an exhibition match after the Mills cup match, W. Warren beat W. Hughes 31-23.

Jack Davies (Llanhilleth) and W. Warren (Waunlwyd) have qualified for the Monmouthshire junior championship — Davies beat W. Baber (Oakdale) 21-19 and Warren defeated H. Chivers (Llanhilleth) 25-4 in the semi-final.

The final will be refereed by Mr. J. Connelly.

168. Fred Parker in action.

169. Fred Parker, the 1939 Welsh Junior Champion, 5 times Welsh Senior champion, Junior and Senior champion of Monmouthshire. He played his first international in 1939.

170. Origin of picture unknown.

171. Origin of picture unknown.

172. Origin of picture unknown.

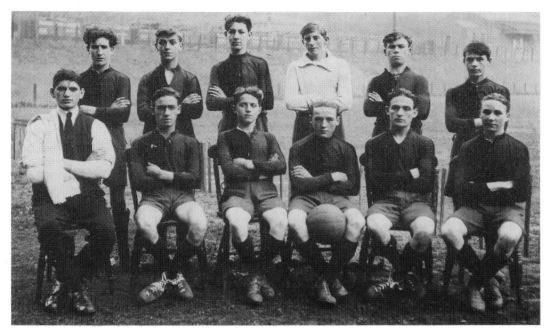

173. Origin of picture unknown.

174. This picture is of Aberbeeg R.F.C., the winners of the Western Valley League in 1919-20. Back row left to right: T. Thomas (Trainer), C. Wilde, W. Beams, G. King, W. Griffiths, T. David, Coun. J. Jones (Chairman), I. Saunders, W. Davies, L. Richards, B. Fox, A. Powell, F. Thatcher, H. Lewis, W.R. Brown (Secretary). Middle row left to right: T. Thomas, A Taylor, O. Richards, T. Davies, R. Powell, L. Davies. Front row left to right: I. Weyborne, R. Saunders, J. Parfitt (vice-captain), S. Saunders (Captain), G. Griffiths, I. Bolt, W. Lewis and F. Grail.

175. Aberbeeg R.F.C. Annual Dinner at the Hanbury Hotel, 1950. Back row left to right: Geo. Bryant, R. Coombes, B. Butler, Jones. Middle row left to right: Gerald Boscher, Wanklyn, M. Leyshon, Allan Carter, B. Turner, Bob Fowler, Basil Wills, C. Blacker. Seated left to right: W. Probyn, J. Evans, J. Clark, A. Kimber, C. Lovell, Riley, A. Saunders.

176. Aberbeeg Rugby Football Team 1955/56. First season on new pitch which was formerly a rubbish dump. Back row left to right: Gerald Boucher, Bob Fowler, R. Hall, Tony James, J. Riley. Middle row left to right: B. Jenkins, Harry Rowley, Martin Day. Front row left to right: W. Probyn, A. Pritchard, B. Inch, D. Davies and T. Adams.

177. A presentation to Mr. Riley of New Zealand, at the Hanbury Hotel in 1950. Also in the picture are T. Clark, C. Boucher, A. Kimber and A. Saunders.

178. The New Zealand All Black's visit to Webbs Brewery in 1953.

179. Llanhilleth All Blacks, Cup Winners 1932. Back row left to right: Rowley Jones, Alf Baber, Dan Morgan. Third row left to right: Alf Davies, Cliff Morgan, Roy Johnson, Jack Challenger, Dick Jones, Harold Jones, Wilf Davies (Trainer). Second row left to right: Gag. Jones, Jack Davies, Lou Morgan, Harry Taylor, Albert Butler, Ted Chivers. Front row left to right: George Sheppard, Len Preece, Reg Blanchard, Harold Thayer.

180.   Llanhilleth Stars.

181.   Llanhilleth R.F.C., 1920.

182. Trinant R.F.C. in their first season, 1956/57. Back row left to right: David Davies, Haydn Rees, Gwyn Powell, Geoff Cattey, Harry Davies, Harry Rowley, John Beckett, Michael Rees, Colin Ricketts, Martyn Day. Front row left to right: Jim Smith, Glyn Morgan, Ian Smith, Howell Jenkins and Alan Jones.

183. Llanhilleth Reserves R.F.C. 1912-13. Back row left to right: M.R. Smith, A. Morgan, H. Edwards, A. Lane, T. Kempthorne, D. Pritchard, J. Prothero, F.J. Hall. Middle row left to right: J.E. Williams (Hon. Sec.), L. Poulton, J. Dare, W. Trump (Capt.), W. Thayer, D. Harris, A. Hewings, H. Whitney. Front row left to right: G. Whitney, W.J. Thayer (Trainer), F. Adams.

184. Llanhilleth Rugby Football Club, 1911-12.

185. Aberbeeg R.F.C. Cyrus Davies Cup winners 1935-36. F. Hall (trainer),
J. Slocombe, S. Cooper, A. Gardner, J. Hollyfield, C.B. Williams, J.R. Clarke
(secretary), J. Gardner, A. Kibby, C. Lane, E. Williams (Captain), W. Clarke,
A. Newman, K. Adams, F. Roan, G. O'Neill, M. Chaplin, J. Slocombe.

186. Llanhilleth Institute Committee. Back row left to right: D. Johns, Tom Morgan, B. Hancock, T. Self, J. Summers, Buller Jeffries, S. Davies, Reg Bennett, Costain, L. Hodder. Front row left to right: E. Donald, H. Dyer, E. Nichols, T. Price, R. Rice (Chairman), B. Smith, Dai Stonuary, J. Phelps.

187. Llanhilleth R.F.C. 1966/67. Standing left to right: M. Sweet, N. Sansom, T. Minchin, J. Sweet, J. Thomas, J. Jones, M. Doyle, A. Parker. Seated left to right: G. Attwell, D. Edwards, M. Crees (Captain), M. Yates, B. Collier. Squatting left to right: C. Burgwin and G. Hewins.

188. Llanhilleth R.F.C., 1957/58. Ben Francis Cup Winners. Back row left to right: J. Mounter, M. Kneads, R. Broom, R. James, Nobby Crozier, H. Beeson, A. Prothero, B. Samson, G. Hibble, Unknown, D. Bryan. Third row left to right: M. Whitlock, D. Watts, J. Crozier, Wiltshire, J. Watkins, T. Wilkie, T. Morgan, J. Beard, B. Jones. Second row left to right: R. Attwell, L. Hagland, D. Jones, Jack Carey (Captain), Jim Creed, R. Jones, T. Verrier. Front row left to right: R. Rogers and I. Pritchard.

189. Llanhilleth R.F.C. Back row left to right: Jack Beard, Malcolm Whitlock, Trevor Morgan, Trevor Holbrook, Colin Evans, Viv Davies, Arthur Hayman, Dennis Iley. Front row left to right: Dennis Watts, Len Chivers, Tony Verrier, Arthur Crozier (Captain), Len Hagland, Tony Wilkins, Jack Watkins.

190. Llanhilleth R.F.C. Mini Rugby Squads (Under 8's and Under 11's) 1980. Standing left to right: Viv Davies, Jonathan Davies, Justin Hodges, Michael Hassal, Ronald Baker, Michael Collier, Wayne Bennett, Shaun Hall, Robert Jones, Richard Brown, Steven Young, Andrew Goode, Jeffrey Dugmore, Michael Mogford, Barry Wall, Anthony Hibbs, Lesley Price. Kneeling left to right: Roddy Morgan, Shane Jones, Darran Bennett, Jason Hale, John Harris, Jason Jones, Andrew Bunn, David Long, Michael Beard, Michael Price. Sitting left to right: Glen Denness, Paul Edwards, Justin Brown, Timothy Allen, Simon Richardson, Graham Jones, Lyn Hagland, David Perry, Patrick O'Connell.

191. Llanhilleth R.F.C. Season 1973/74. Standing left to right: M. Butler, M. Williams, R. Addison, J. O'Connell, A. Higgins, D. Rogers, D. Williams, S. Rogers, M. Crees, B. Purnell, D. Powell. Seated left to right: H. Brown, B. Pidgeon, J. Griffiths, C. James, R. Lewis (Capt.), T. Dalton, N. Thomas, B. Collier. Squatting left to right: E. Newman, L. Rogers and G. Weaver.

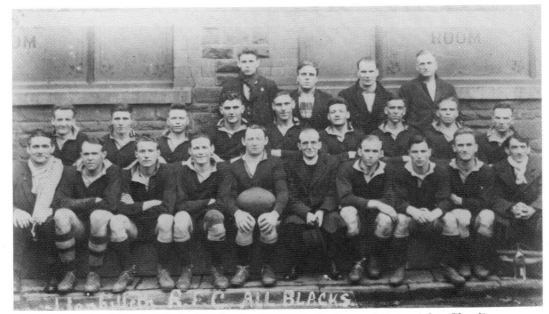

192. Llanhilleth R.F.C. All Blacks, 1930/31. Back row left to right: Charlie Galton, Harry Taylor, Charlie Jones. Middle row left to right: C. Phillips, G. Jones, D. Lucas, R. Belcher, Gill Morgan, A. Butler, Len Preece, John Jones, Dick Jones. Front row left to right: B. Davies, Cliff Morgan, Harold Thayer, Sam Smith, T. Chivers, Rev. Madog Williams, Lou Morgan, Geo. Sheppard, Eddie Jones and A. Davies.

193. Llanhilleth All Blacks 1905/06. Fifth from left in the centre row is R. Williams.

194. Llanhilleth Quins R.F.C. Runners-up in the Blaina Hospital Cup 1935/36. In the picture are Bill Preston Jnr., C. Lewis, E. Morgan, M. Neads, D. Butcher, G. Williams, Ike Mounter, D. Jones, B. Preston Snr., J. Jayne, G. Lewis, B. Jayne, J. Kibby, M. Evans, H. Thayer, G. Eatwell, C. Challenger, G. Smithy, H. Jayne, Snowy Griffiths, D. Lewis, R. Lucas, A. Prothero, T. Thomas, H. Lane, A. Snook and Benson.

195. 1938 Harlequins R.F.C. outing to Scotland. Back row left to right: T. Thomas, L. Morgan, Merlin Meads, G. Williams, E. Roberts, Snook. Front row left to right: D. Thomas, M. Evans, W. Preston, A. Prothero, C. Lewis and I. Mounter.

196. Llanhilleth R.F.C., Cyrus Davies Cup Winners 1951/52. Back row left to right: I. Trimm, G. Smithey, D. Bryan, R. Smith, B. Lewis, B. Goff, S. Terret. Third row left to right: C. Burchell, W. Coleman, A. Prothero, S. Butler, J. Davies, T. Jones, H. Beeson. Second row left to right: D. Lewis, G. Angel, L. Carey, R. Williams, R. Catlin, J. Watkins, R. Plaister, E. Hopkins, J. Coleman, C. Prosser. Seated left to right: B. Jones, J. Morgan, E. Pople (Chairman), D. Jones (Captain), W. Preston (Sec.), S. Norris, N. Morgan (Llanhilleth's only Welsh International, played for Wales in 1960). Squatting left to right: G. Jeffries and P. Williams.

CHAPTER 11

and finally ...

197. Back row left to right: D. Helps, A. Sutton, D. Davies, D. Summers. Middle row: H. Cowley, B. Long, B. Jones, B. Morris. Front row: D. Pope, T. Poyner, H. Davies, R. Brimble.

198. 1955 Carnival. Maureen Evans, Elaine Morgan and Marion Pound.

199. Penyfan Pond 1928.

200. Troy Road, street party.

201. 1951 Festival of Britain, Meadow Street party with waitress, Mrs. R. Rice.

202. Carnival time in Railway Street.

203. Mr. Edmund (Peggy) Jones feeding chickens at the rear of Blaencuffin Road on the mountain.

204. Postman Harry Holmes and his transport.

205. Llanhilleth T.A.s, World War 2.

206. Carnival Time
at Hafodarthen.

207. Llanhilleth Rugby Club celebration dinner at the Central Hotel. Amongst those present were (?) Butler and Dick Lewis.

208. The staff of the roll turning division at the John Paton Tinworks in Abertillery. The firm used to make tin for containers used in a variety of industries. The men in the photograph are (top row left to right) A. Lambert, R. Kirkpatrick, C. Parry, D. Evans, L. Rees, C. Saunders, A. Williams and W. Morris. In the front row are R. Saunders, C. Robins, W. Prosser, A. Kirkpatrick, J. English and T. Burgam.

209. Oxford Street tea party, with Mrs. Summers in the centre of the photograph holding a baby.

210. Aberbeeg Hospital celebration. Sister Lewis shaking hands with Matron Body. Looking on, third from the right in the back row is Sister Longhurst who became Matron of Nevill Hall Hospital.

211. Llanhilleth Rugby Celebration Dinner at the Central Hotel. Sitting at the top table left to right: David Jones, Mr. Creed, Doug Jones, Mrs. Jones, Bill Preston and Marie Preston.

212. Oxford Street tea party. Mrs. Summers is fourth from the right at the back.

213. Llanhilleth Hotel, early 1900.

214. Zion Congregational Chapel and Schools, Llanhilleth.

215. Llanhilleth Colliery. Some of the high quality coal can be seen here.

216. Llanhilleth from the railway station.

217. Llanhilleth Collieries, showing the extensive rail facilities.

218. Llanhilleth, view down valley. Llanhilleth Colliery, Havod-y-coed Houses, Dust Hole House near railway line.

CHAPTER 12

Tradespeople in Aberbeeg and Llanhilleth. Circa 1934

Commercial Road

No. 2   Eastmans, Butcher
No. 2A   Isaac Levy, Outfitter
No. 4   India & China Tea Co. Grocers
No. 5   H. Woodley & Co., Butcher
No. 6   Lemuel Jones, Butcher
No. 8   Caple Marks, Greengrocer
Nos. 9/11   Hunt Bros., Saddlers
No. 12   Fredrick Beechey, Ironmonger
No. 13   Alex Buchan, Tailor
No. 14   Adams & Son, Greengrocer
No. 15   Wm. Holmes, Confectioner
No. 19   Edward Head, Confectioner
No. 21   Wm. Burchell, Newsagent
No. 23   S.R.K. Thomas MPS, Chemist
No. 25   Arthur Thomas, Greengrocer
No. 31   Midland Bank
No. 33   Albert Thomas, Butcher
No. 35   Mrs. J. Smith, Draper
No. 37   Phillip Taylor, Tailor
No. 48   Miss. M. Addis, Shopkeeper
No. 52   Edith Carter, Fried Fish Dealer
Station Chambers Caefelin Building Co.
Geo. Boscott, Cycle Dealer
William Dicks, Baker
Gorman & Son, Estate Agents
Albert Paget, Newsagent
Peglers Ltd., Grocer

High Street

No. 1A   Victor A. Thomas, Grocer
No. 4   Mrs. Doris Rees, Wireless Supplies
No. 4   J. Edgar Smith, Sweetshop
No. 4   Mrs. Rachael Bowen, Confectioner
No. 6   James Bartlett, Grocer
No. 12   Jack Morgan, Hairdresser
No. 12A Stanley Godwin, Outfitter
No. 13A G. Paull, Music Warehouse
No. 14   Albert Dykes, Greengrocer
No. 15   Wm. Hayes, Shopkeeper
No. 16   Wm. Herbert, Provision Dealer
No. 18   Chas. M. Saunders, Dentist
No. 18   Mrs. Alice Saunders, Shopkeeper
No. 20   Mrs. Mary Hutton, Shopkeeper

No. 23   John. Carter, Haulier
No. 28   Harold Cousins, Cycle Agent & Dealer
Wesleyan Bldgs. Jn. Anderson, Wireless Eng.
Wesleyan Bldgs. Gwyn D. Sykes, Corn Merchant
Wesleyan Bldgs. Percy Thayer, Hairdresser
4 Wesleyan Bldgs. Miss Ruby Downs, Draper
Blaina & Ind. & Provident Society Limited
Charles Dayton, Shopkeeper
Joseph Flook, Boot Repairer
Lionel Thomas, Grocer
Wm. Wheeler, Plumber
Fredrick Rawlinson, Stationer

Hotels, Inns and Clubs

The Central Hotel, Wm. Sheldrake
The Walpole Hotel, Wm. Phillips
Llanhilleth Hotel, Harry Lewis
Hanbury Hotel, Howard Collins
Llanhilleth Con. & Unionist Club, C.E. Cole, Sec.
Royal Oak Hotel, John Hall
Aberbeeg Social Club & Institute, R. Bowen, Sec.
Carpenters Arms, Mrs. M. Hunt
Castle Inn, J. Parfitt

Shopkeepers in Llanhilleth

Mrs. M. Beard, Shopkeeper, 42 Railway St.
Miss L. Bridges, Shopkeeper, 5 Blaencuffin Road
Mrs. M. Burton, Shopkeeper, 43 Meadow Street
Mrs. E. Carter, Shopkeeper, 20 Caefelin Street
Danish Butter Co., Shopkeeper, 2 Railway Street
Mrs. E. Fry, Shopkeeper, 16 Railway Street
Miss. R. Gabb, Shopkeeper, 2 Partridge Road
Mr. J. George, Shopkeeper, 9 Andrew Terrace
Mr. W. Graill, Shopkeeper, Brynithel
Mrs. N. Griffiths, Shopkeeper, 33 Hafodarthen Rd.
Mr. E. Humphreys, Shopkeeper, 4 Partridge Rd.
Mrs. M. Jones, Shopkeeper, 16 Penygraig Tce.
Mrs. M. Jones, Shopkeeper, 1 Meadow Street
Mrs. M. Jones, Shopkeeper, 6 Bronheulog Tce.
Mr. H. Kibby, Shopkeeper, 69 Meadow Street
Mrs. M. Matthews, Shopkeeper, 41 Partridge Rd.
Mr. A. Phillips, Shopkeeper, 72 Meadow Street

Mr. J. Harris, Shopkeeper, Brooklyn Terrace
Mrs. G. Purnell, Shopkeeper, 24 Central Road
Mrs. E. Reid, Fish Shop, Hafodarthen Road
Miss. E. Snook, Shopkeeper, 32 Hafodarthen Rd.
Mrs. S. Summers, Shopkeeper, 2 Troy Road

Shopkeepers in Aberbeeg

Mrs. F. Parfitt, Shopkeeper
Miss V. Bell, Shopkeeper, 16 Aberbeeg Road
James Edgar Bolt, Blacksmith
David R. Davies, Dairyman
Mrs. Ellinor Day, Baker (James & Day)
Courtney Edmunds, Grocer
Leslie Hale, Shopkeeper, 17 Old Woodland Tce.
David Jenkins, Postmaster
Fred Jones, Hairdresser
Henry Kibby, Provision Dealer
Joseph Lewis, Shopkeeper, 10 Glandwr St.
R. Lewis, Butcher, Commercial Square
L. Lloyd, Butcher, Belmont
J. Martindale, Painter, Elmlea Pantddu Road
J. Rowlands, Ironmonger
W. Thomas & Son, Provision Merchants
L. Poole, Newsagent, The Square
Thos. Miles, Mortar Merchant, Glandwr
Webbs, Brewery

Doctors

L.S. Frost, M.B., Ch.B. Edin
T.J. Frost, L.R.C.P. Edin, L.R.C.S., L.M.Edin, L.R.F.P.S.
W.R. Scanlon, F.R.C.S. Edin, L.R.C.P., M.R.C.S., D.T.M. & H.

CHAPTER 13

The Aberbeeg Tragedy

by Howard Williams

This was the dramatic headline in a local newspaper on July 15, 1911. It referred to an incident which was without precedent in Monmouthshire and which, fortunately, is unique in the annals of the Force - the slaying of a police officer, P.C.142 Hosea Pope who was stationed at Aberbeeg.

Before the First World War the strength of the County Constabulary was about one fifth of the present number. The disposition of that Force was interesting. There was, for example, an inspector in charge at Blaina and Abertillery, and an inspector and two constables were stationed at the County Police Station, Pentonville, Newport. Also, at Risca there was a superintendent, sergeant, and about half a dozen constables.

At this time communications were, in the main, pedestrian or perhaps equestrian. There was no telephone system between out-stations and sub-divisional stations, and crimes or disturbances in out-station areas had, for the first few hours, to be dealt with by the local officer, alone and unaided.

Aberbeeg police station is a Victorian building typical of hundreds throughout Britain and was obviously built with an eye for the future. At various times a sergeant and a constable had been stationed there; but, in 1911 the station constable - P.C. Pope - was the only officer.

Hosea Pope joined the Monmouthshire Constabulary on January 13th, 1903, after service in the Grenadier Guards. He was then twenty five years old. He had enjoyed being a soldier and had served in South Africa throughout the Boer War. At the end of the war having been in the army for five and a half years he decided to leave and join his local police force.

A native of Llanmartin he hoped to be posted to a country area near his home. This, however, was not to be. After training at Abergavenny he was posted to Abertillery. Three years later he was transferred to Aberbeeg; and, as a single man, he lived in the police station with the constable-in-charge and his wife.

In 1910 he married Emily Haines, a Llanmartin girl, ten years his junior, whom he had known for some years. After the marriage P.C. Pope moved into the main living quarters of the station and became the constable-in-charge at Aberbeeg.

Aberbeeg at that time was busy and prosperous. Several hundred men were employed at the colliery on Cwm Road (the present day site of the Brondeg filling station), at Webb's brewery, and at the Great Western Railway depot. There was also a great deal of drinking with the Hanbury Hotel and the Ivorites Hotel selling considerably more beer (at four pence a pint) than is usual today.

There were many fights and PC Pope often had the cells of his station full because the town was as rough as any similar sized place in the valleys.

However, Hosea Pope was not a man to be trifled with. He was almost six feet tall and was very strong; and, although he was known as a decent man and was well respected in the area, it was generally accepted that he could handle all the rough-necks in the town.

One such rogue was James Wise a native of Blaina. He lived, (when he had money) in a lodging house in Alma Street, Abertillery. At other times he was either an inmate of Tredegar workhouse or he slept rough in the area.

He was thirty seven years old, about five feet six inches tall and of slight build. Wise, who was usually seen with a few days growth of beard, was frequently involved in violence. He had served several prison sentences and was in the habit of accosting children on their way to Arrael Street School and stealing their sandwiches!

He had never been known to be in regular employment, but, occasionally delivered sawdust to local public houses. On days when he did not feel like the walk back to Abertillery after a night in Aberbeeg he would sleep in gardens and out-buildings. This of course would usually result in a complaint to P.C. Pope from the householder.

Like many others of that type Wise was in frequent contact (and usually conflict) with the law, which in his eyes was personified by P.C. Pope, P.C. Birch, of Six Bells and P.C. Pritchard of Abertillery.

Later evidence would be given that, on or about July 10, while drinking with his cronies, in the Rolling Mill public house Wise had stated his intention of 'putting them through it' if he ever 'met them in a quiet place.' Witnesses would also say that he had threatened P.C. Pope on other occasions.

P.C. Hosea Pope

On July 14th, 1911, Wise had spent the evening at the Ivorites Hotel. At 10.30 p.m. he was standing outside the worse for drink, despite the fact that the Hotel had closed at 10 p.m. Meanwhile, P.C. Pope had left Aberbeeg police station at 10 p.m. He was about to work a night shift, and he told his wife, who was now two months pregnant, that he would return for his meal break about 1 a.m. This was the last time Mrs. Pope was to see her husband alive.

P.C. Pope was in the habit of ensuring that the licensed premises in the area had emptied and that all was peaceful. Thus, when he arrived at the Ivorites Hotel he came across Wise and after an altercation he apparently decided to escort Wise from the area.

At the time P.C. Pope was dealing with Wise, two young men, Henry Parfitt and Jim Green, were walking slowly along the road from Aberbeeg Square. They were returning to their homes in Warm Turn, Aberbeeg, after an evening at Llanhilleth Playhouse.

About 10.40 p.m. when the men were halfway up the hill Henry heard footsteps behind him, and suddenly felt a tap on his shoulder. He turned and saw P.C. Pope. The officer was holding a man by the arm but, because there were no street lights, neither Henry nor Jim could later say if the man was handcuffed. However, both recognised the man, it was Jimmy Wise.

P.C. Pope apparently felt the need to reassure the two young men because he said 'it's alright, lads, don't follow too closely.' He and Wise then walked on up the hill. The two young men thought no more about the incident. To them Wise had apparently been up to something and was now either under arrest or was being escorted out of Aberbeeg. Henry and Jim reached their homes and bade each other goodnight.

Later, about 11 p.m. when Henry was eating his supper, a Mr. Brown came to the front door and excitedly told him that a policeman was lying across the pavement at Warm Turn and that he seemed to be dead.

Mr. Brown said that he had been returning from Abertillery and when he had reached Arrael Street School he had met P.C. Pope and Wise. Pope was standing over Wise, who was lying on the footpath. His helmet was about ten yards away and both men appeared exhausted.

'The constable, who was bleeding profusely from a wound over his left eye, called upon Brown to assist him in arresting Wise. He then told Brown that Wise had struck him with a large stone which was lying on the ground nearby. (This would later be recovered by Inspector Lewis and was found to weigh 12 1/2 ounces and to have traces of blood, skin and hair upon it).

Brown assisted P.C. Pope who placed handcuffs on Wise's left hand, and the three started walking back towards Aberbeeg. Wise had earlier said to P.C. Pope, 'Mind, I'll pay you for this', and a short time after the three had set off he wrenched his right arm away from Brown and struck the P.C. a hard blow in the face. Pope fell backwards onto the ground and did not move. Wise immediately took to his heels and ran off towards Six Bells still with the handcuffs on his left wrist.'

Brown and Henry Parfitt ran to the scene and found P.C. Pope in the position Brown had described. In the light of a lamp which other people

now at the scene had brought it could be seen that P.C. Pope's face and almost all the front of his tunic was covered in blood.

It was obvious to all that he was dead. He was carried into the house next to the school, while Dr. Sullivan of Six Bells was sent for, and Mr. Brown ran to Abertillery police station to get assistance.

The police arrived quite quickly. When events like this occurred it was surprising how rapidly word would travel from place to place even without the aid of telephones - perhaps proving the old adage 'bad news has good legs'. In the event the first policeman on the scene was P.C. Birch of Six Bells, who was followed soon afterwards by Inspector Lewis of Abertillery with a sergeant and a constable.

After brief enquiries, and the information given by Mr. Brown, everyone present knew that the killer was Jimmy Wise and, as the newspapers were to say the following day, 'a hue and cry was raised.'

The police officers, assisted enthusiastically by most of the Lower Six Bells populace, began systematically to search the area (including the gardens) of Lancaster Street, Lancaster Villas, Arrael Street, Upper Arrael Street and Griffin Street.

Meanwhile the body of P.C. Pope, having been certified as dead by Dr. Sullivan was carried to Aberbeeg Post Office which was next door to the police station. Mrs. Jenkins, the wife of the postmaster was friendly with Mrs Pope and it was thought that in view of Mrs Pope's condition she should not be given the terrible news until the morning.

The search for Wise continued in Six Bells, where the residents of Griffin Street were on their doorsteps awaiting the arrival of the police. Mr Mortimer of number 1 was there with his brother-in-law, Mr Parker, who lived next door when they were suddenly approached by Wise who emerged from an alley that led to Arrael Street.

Wise first asked if he could sleep in the toilet of Mr Mortimer's house. Then, on being refused, he held up his hand and showed the handcuff that was dangling from it. He said, 'I'm covered in blood, I had a set to with a policeman, but I outed the b.......' The men now knew that this was the killer.

They immediately changed their attitude towards Wise and Mr Mortimer told him to go through to the kitchen and wash. As Wise did so Mr Parker ran to tell the police search party. Mr Mortimer meanwhile followed Wise to the kitchen and while engaging him in conversation he 'gave him a glass of shandygaff which seemed to calm him.'

After a short time P.C. Birch and a number of local people entered the house and went through to the kitchen. There, according to contemporary newspaper accounts 'a desperate struggle took place' in which eight people eventually became involved in trying to handcuff Wise. At last he was subdued and was taken from the house to Abertillery Police Station.

'Although it was never brought out in the newspaper coverage or during the subsequent trial, there was a strong belief that Wise was all along under the impression that the policeman who had arrested him and whom he had subsequently killed was P.C. Birch of Six Bells.

Apparently Wise had fallen foul of P.C. Birch more

often than he had of P.C. Pope. Also, on the morning of July 14th he had been moved from the vicinity of Arrael Street School by P.C. Birch. Thus, when later that night, P.C. Pope was escorting him past that school, and an opportunity to escape had presented itself, he may have thought he was dealing with P.C. Birch.

It is said by some that when P.C. Birch entered the house in Upper Griffin Street, Wise began screaming in absolute terror; perhaps being under the impression that this was the man he had killed. However, there is no evidence to support this version of the events and yet it is still regarded as being true by some who remember the incident.'

Wise was detained at Abertillery Police Station where he was interviewed by Inspector Lewis. He was later to tell the Court that Wise, while being searched had said, 'I wouldn't have done this for my right hand.' This was a complete volteface, for, when he had heard that P.C. Pope was dead, he had told Mr Mortimer, 'good job, there's nobody to talk about it now except me.'

The inquest on the officer was held the following day at Aberbeeg Police Station by the coroner, Mr J.B. Walford. Tributes to the dead constable were paid by the Coroner, and the jury. For the police, Inspector Lewis said, 'I can say ... that he was a

Justice Pickford.

During the trial Dr. Sullivan who had performed the post-mortem examination said that P.C. Pope's heart had not been as healthy as it should have been, and apparently the jury felt that this condition had contributed to his death. Also, the Judge asked the jury to consider if an officer could be said to be acting in the execution of his duty when he was 'moving someone on.'

The prosecution tried to counter these arguments by saying that even if the officer was not acting in the execution of his duty it would not justify anyone resorting to assault or, in this case, murder. However it was to no avail. After much legal argument, and submissions by counsel, Wise was convicted of manslaughter and was sentenced to five years penal servitude.

Thus, the case of the 'Aberbeeg Tragedy' was closed. The life of an excellent constable only thirty three years old, and looking forward to the arrival of his first child, had been cruelly and prematurely ended.

It is no doubt easy to comment with hindsight; but surely, had Dr. Sullivan not placed such stress on the fact of P.C. Pope's slightly enlarged heart the proper charge, murder, would have stood. P.C. Pope's tunic, saturated in blood from the officer's facial wounds,

Aberbeeg Police Station

constable in whom I had every confidence. He was a very trustworthy and reliable officer.'

A verdict of 'murder' was returned, and on Wednesday, July 26, 1911, Wise appeared before Abertillery Magistrates' Court on remand from Usk Prison. It was then stated that while the train conveying Wise and his single prison warden escort was passing through the tunnel outside Newport railway station Wise had made a determined effort to escape. He had smashed the compartment window and only after a violent struggle had the warden subdued him.

On November 10, 1911, Wise appeared at the Monmouthshire Assizes, held at Monmouth before Mr.

was produced in court. Yet, these wounds were dealt with in no great detail.

The main discussion at the trial was the condition of the victim's heart; and, whether he had the right, outside the Ivorites Hotel, to move his assailant on. However eighty years later, it is hard to understand why Wise was not found guilty of murder as charged.'

People frequently talk of 'the good old days' when the police had the full backing of the courts and a substantial majority of the people. Yet as we have seen, at the trials of the day academic arguments, far removed from the realities of the outside world, and the circumstances of the particular incident were, it seems, as prevalent as they are today.